HOW TO
UNDERSTAND MEN

Emotional Availability, Attraction, and Getting
Him to Obsess Over You

By K. Connors

INTRODUCTION

Do you find it difficult to understand your man? How do your conversations end? Doesn't he want you to want him too? Or do you find it hard to do what he wants you to do? Yes, most women find it very challenging to understand men. Most women think men are more complicated than anything else in the world, thus leading to breakups.

It's funny how men find it difficult to understand women and women find it difficult to understand men. However, there are ways for these two individuals to meet halfway. Women can still understand what men think and what men say. You just simply need to learn how to read the clues and the signs. Once you do, your relationships will be better and stronger.

Men are not as difficult to understand as some might think. Read on and you will find useful tips to understand what men want to say and what men want you to do. Knowing how to understand men is one important thing that most women long for, but don't always succeed on the first try. Women sometimes have trouble with not being understood in relationships, but often neglect about how to understand men in their lives.

CHAPTER 1

HOW TO UNDERSTAND MEN

Knowing how to understand men is one important thing that women need to keep in mind. Women sometimes think of not being understood in a relationship - but often neglect about how to understand men in their lives. In the end, we sometimes find our spouses cheating on us and not understanding why. So early on, let us try to decipher what men really want from women.

WHY ARE MEN SO ENGROSSED WITH SEX?

Men's sexual drive is indeed different from that of a woman. The hormone testosterone in the man is responsible for wanting sex, as caused by their libido. Thus, it is but normal for men to be constantly looking for sex. If you want to understand men and their sex drives, you might also want to understand that they have different feelings towards sex because of the testosterone pressure they feel in their bodies. In relationships, many women seek attention; for love and pampering and men tend to be seeking for sex. Knowing these differences and understanding why these differences exist, will truly help you in how to please your partner to make them happy in marriage.

MEN NEED SPACE FOR THEMSELVES

This goes the same for women as well. We all need space in our lives. Being in a relationship or tying the knot with the man you love does not necessarily mean clinging to that man day after day. Sometimes when women are so overwhelmed and in love, they tend to love having their man around and spending time with him, but need to understand that sometimes men want to have their quiet time or time with friends. Just because you are married, doesn't mean you always have to tag along with your man anywhere he goes. In marriage, you can manage this by giving time for him to be by himself and schedule time for you to spend together. Although too much space for both of you can also be bad for the relationship, so it is important to create balance.

MEN NEED TIME TO THINK

You may probably get upset when you are trying to bring up a concern and your man doesn't seem to respond to it immediately. Sometimes, women think men are not interested in what they regarding issues that are brought to their attention. To women, it seems like he may be thinking about something else, which sometimes can end up in an argument in itself. It is important to understand that most often, men want to process their problems and their thoughts to themselves, and they may want to think about it for some time. Oftentimes, men want to talk about it when they are able to come up with a solution, as opposed to talking about it piece by piece.

These are just three ways on how to understand men in your life. There are still a lot of differences between men and women that somehow we need to understand to help us build a good relationship with our significant other. So, the next time you get upset or angry, take the time to put yourself in their shoes and try to understand how they're thinking about it and their behavior towards the situation.

CHAPTER 2

WHAT THE MAJORITY OF MEN LOOK FOR IN WOMEN

When it comes to relationship issues, many men ajust aren't as savvy as women. When encountered with a problem, women will search for an answer be it through relationship manuals or advice columns, and even take advice from friends who also have relationship problems. Some men spend time protecting their egos rather than allowing themselves to be honest about what they really want in a relationship. In reality, deep down, men want the same things as the majority of women. That is to find a lifelong partner, a soul mate, someone to love and be loved in return by a person who makes their hearts flutter uncontrollably. To have a long and happy life and to grow old with that special person. Men long to find a woman who can stimulate them romantically, emotionally and intellectually.

HERE ARE SOME OF THE QUALITIES A MAN LOOKS FOR IN A WOMAN.

Men are attracted to a woman who exudes both sensuality and femininity and who makes the imagination run wild. The male instinct is to look for all potential partners as long term mates and look for a woman they feel will be loyal and trustworthy.

Women love to be seduced and men are no different. Men like to think they are in charge and want a woman who can let them be strong, even after she is aware of their weaknesses. It is not in a man's psychological makeup to admit to not being able to handle any situation, so they need a woman who can make them stronger than they can be on their own.

One thing that is very common in men is fear of commitment. Men can go into battle to fight wars, swim with sharks or jump out of a plane, but the thought of being with one woman for the rest of our lives induces some kind of uncontrollable fear.

Men like having options. They might think they are ready to settle down with that special woman they just met, but still leave the possibility open that someone else may come along. However, when a man really does commit, then he will really love and cherish his woman.

Real men appreciate real women. To a man, that is a woman who is strong but who will still allow the man to lead (sometimes), someone who is intelligent but still willing to learn. Someone who understands them and their dreams and who is willing to help them achieve it. And finally, someone sensual, but is loyal and faithful.

It is important for a man to have a woman who contributes to the relationship and does not seek only what she can get out of it. In short, a man wants a feminine, sensual, trustworthy soul mate. This of course doesn't encompass 100% of the men out there, as there are always exceptions.

QUALITIES MEN LOOK FOR IN WOMEN

Asking what qualities men look for in women is a bit like asking what flavors of ice cream they like. Every man will be different, but there will always be a few obvious favorites. To some extent, the qualities men look for in women depend on what the man wants from their partner as they will look for different qualities in a marriage partner than they will for someone to have fun with on a Saturday night. Chocolate Brownie might be their ice cream of choice, but if you're asking them to eat a whole tub, maybe they'd prefer Butter Pecan? With that in mind, here are a few of the usual qualities men look for in women.

We have to start with physical qualities because there's no denying that the initial attraction a man feels towards a woman is likely to be physical. You might be surprised what men find physically attractive. The media would have us believe that men only go for skinny, leggy blondes with enormous breasts, but how many men do you know that have actually ended up with girls like that? An average looking woman that smiles or laughs a lot is generally more attractive to a man than a natural beauty who is permanently sulking or scowling. Finding a style that suits you and accentuates your good points, rather than trying to be something you are not, will make you look great and will increase your confidence; a trait that men find very appealing. Ladies, true beauty lies within your confidence.

Men do appreciate it when women make an effort with their appearance. This doesn't mean you need to cake on the makeup, but if it brings out your good features, knock yourself out. However, worrying about your hairstyle or new shoes getting messed up can stop you from being any fun and that is a real turn off.

Independence can be an attractive quality for some men. Having your own interests and friends, as well as your own ideas and views, can make a woman more interesting to be around. Financial independence is a tricky one, however. If they are entirely honest, a lot of men can't cope with their woman earning more than they do. It's just the traditional ideology that's getting more and more outdated. I say make as much money as you can; men that are threatened by this frankly need to get over it.

To continue with the 1950s stereotype, it is true that men do like to be looked after. Being able to cook a half decent meal, iron his shirts and look after his kids, is something that a man will be looking for in a woman. This may sound old fashioned in the twenty-first century, but that doesn't stop it from being true. Desperation is a really unattractive trait in a woman, so no matter how much you like a guy, or want to get married and have kids, for heaven's sake play it cool. You need to let him know you're interested, but listening to his stories and smiling at him is more effective than stalking him after the first date, or declaring your undying love. Surprisingly, the majority of men are looking to find a partner they can settle down with, but start talking marriage and children and you're in danger of scaring him off. Some men enjoy the chase, while others don't. I prefer the route of being up front, and don't make either one of you do most of the running.

Overall, men are looking for women that are cheerful, positive, and fun to be around. No guy is going to stick around for long if you are constantly complaining, even if you do look like a supermodel. Being adventurous and willing to try new things is a very attractive quality, but don't be scared to be a little weak or vulnerable; most men like to feel they can protect their women. You may feel that no man will ever find you attractive, but consider a few of these simple rules and you'll be fighting off the admirers.

CHAPTER 3

WHAT IS ATTRACTIVE TO MOST MEN?

What is attractive to men? That's the one question every woman wishes she knew the answer to. Some women struggle with understanding exactly how to appeal to the guy they're interested in. They take their cues from what they see around them and that's not always the best path to take, however logical it may seem. If you try and transform yourself into what you think he wants, based on what the media is suggesting men want, you may find yourself alone and confused. There are specific qualities that men are naturally drawn to within a woman. Focus on these and he'll be chasing after you in no time.

HERE ARE QUALITIES THAT MEN FIND IRRESISTIBLE IN A WOMAN:

1.   A SENSE OF HUMOR:

Men want to have fun and they love to laugh. They long to be with someone who doesn't take life too seriously and who is willing to laugh at the world around her and herself. Find your sense of humor and embrace it. He'll love being around you if you always make him smile. You don't have to be a comedian, just show that you love life and love to have a good time. Smiling and laughing is one of the best ways to show this.

2.   SELF-ACCEPTANCE:

You'll never be perfect. None of us ever will be. That's just a fact of life. If you want to make yourself attractive to a particular man, just accept the woman you are, flaws and all. If you're not constantly making excuses for the way you look, your attitude or what you do for a living, he'll find that very appealing. Men are used to interacting with women who try and excuse away their shortcomings. Don't do that!

3.   GENUINE COMPASSION:

To most men, one quality that an ideal woman will always possess is compassion. They envision their future partner to have a heart of gold and to always put others before themself. Be kind to everyone, every day. Not only will this show him that you're a genuinely good person, it will make you feel great about yourself too.

4.   HONESTY:

You may think that you can get away with telling a white lie to your guy but you won't. Men can see through a false front in no time, whether they reveal it or not. He wants to know that he can always trust you and that means that you have to be honest with him 100% of the time.

5.   THE SENSE OF ADVENTURE:

No, this doesn't mean that you have to be willing to go skydiving with him. But you should be open to the idea of a fun and interesting adventure from time-to-time. If you're not one for spur of the moment change, you may actually turn him off. Men crave to be with someone who is ready to jump in the car at a moment's notice and go explore parts unknown. Show him that spontaneity is your middle name and he'll want to spend as much time with you as he can. Always ensure your best qualities shine through when you are trying to win the attention and adoration of a special man. If you push aside all those self-doubts, the real you will shine through and he won't be able to resist you.

CHAPTER 4

THE FIRST DATE, WHAT TO EXPECT OR DO

So Prince Charming has finally asked you out. You've been desperately trying to get his attention. You finally did and now you have a date planned. You're so excited that you can hardly stand it. Then come the flood of questions that run through your mind. What am I going to wear? What should I do with my hair? Where will we go? What will we do?

And then comes the biggest one of all... what are we going to talk about? Did you know that one of the most important first date tips for women involves the conversation and what you talk about during the date? It's true and the reason is because it is what captures a man's attention most. Don't get me wrong. You do want to look good, even hot. But your looks will only take you so far as to get the first date. From there, it's what you say that will leave him wanting more. Now the question becomes, "What can I say to nail the first date and clinch a second?" This is the dating advice you really need, so pay close attention.

First dates can never be forgotten, you will remember your first date throughout your whole life. At first, first dates can really build up a sweat in you. You could be shy and not talk much which could also be reasons why your second date with the same person might never take off. On the other hand, you could be really talkative and not let the other speak, over confident, etc., which is not what the other person might expect. This could be another reason why you could blow up your first date. If you want to make sure that your first date is not only memorable, but lands you the chance on a second one, then there are a few pointers that you might want to consider. Although these are not foolproof, they will surely give you the right amount of confidence and you will be your perfect best.

1. CLEAN UP

Make sure that you take a bath or shower and don't forget to spray up some perfume or cologne. It is important that you are clean and smell decent too. Guys need to make sure they don't turn up unshaven or looking frumpy. Women, don't look ratchet. You don't want to look messy on your first date. The first impression is the last impression in this case.

2. WHERE TO GO?

Suggest to your partner that you have your date in a restaurant, a movie theater, picnic area, or any venue where there are other people around. This way, your date cannot get too cozy with you. Spending time together where you are given too much privacy is not a good idea to spend your first date. As a woman, you need to think of your safety first. It's also good to participate in an ongoing activity like bowling, miniature golf, etc., as awkward silences are almost inevitable in a stagnant environment.

3. WHAT TO WEAR?

Do not wear provocative clothing as you will be sending the wrong message to your date. This does not mean that you should wear "granny" clothes to show that you are a conservative type. The point is to dress attractively, not promiscuously.

4. WHAT TO TALK ABOUT?

Most men expect women to start the conversation first. Whether you like it or not, this is just how it is. If your date is the quiet type, then you may feel pressured to keep talking just so avoid deafening silence. But make sure that you strike an intelligent conversation. Do not just babble about anything and everything under the sun. First date tips for women would tell you not to monopolize the conversation. Do not talk too much about yourself. Give him a chance to talk about himself as well.

5. BE INTERESTING

This does not mean you hog up the entire conversation and talk about yourself all the time. First dates are a great time to know if you've made the right choice; it's the time for meaningful conversations where you get to know each other's likes and dislikes. Don't steal the limelight and talk about yourself unless asked. Make sure that you give your date a chance to talk about themselves too. Get to know everything that is relevant like hobbies, favorites, family, etc. This will keep the conversation interesting and you will have a wonderful time. In fact, this is just the tip of the iceberg, and you will unknowingly pave the way for a second date.

6. BE THERE ON TIME

Just like an interview (this is essentially what a first date is), it is important that you turn up for your first date on time or else you will only send out the wrong signal. Make sure that you inform your date in case you are held up somewhere and it could take you some time to get there, that way your date won't feel abandoned.

Women love to keep their men waiting, it's best that you don't overdo it though, a few minutes late is understandable, but nothing beyond that.

7. CHOOSE AN ACTIVITY YOU ENJOY

On the first date, you should choose an activity that you honestly enjoy. If you choose an activity that you hate, but you think your date will enjoy, your body language may give up the ruse you are trying to pull. However, if you do something you like, your attitude will be great without you having to worry about it.

TIPS FOR WOMEN ON HOW TO LOOK YOUR BEST ON YOUR FIRST DATE

When it comes to first dates, appearance matters. The way you dress and present yourself to your date will speak volumes about your character, whether the conversation is flowing freely or not. This is equally true for both men and women, and the first impressions your date gleans from your appearance may make the difference between a second date and a brush-off. When you meet someone for the first time, you no doubt pay close attention to his or her appearance, whether consciously or sub-consciously. This includes things like clothing, hairstyle, and odor, and in the absence of much other information about the person sitting across from us, these little clues are what we go on to assess their suitability as a potential partner. Needless to say, whilst you sit there quietly judging this perfect or not so perfect stranger, your date is doing the same.

So what can you do to ensure that your appearance makes for a favorable first impression on your date?

1. MAKE-UP- LESS IS MORE

Most men like a woman who looks good with make-up on, but they also want to know that when the makeup comes off, what's underneath is just as appealing. Wearing too much make-up also runs the risk of ruining the skin underneath and may indicate to your date that you're a little lax in your skincare routine.

2. SKIN

A good skin care regime is important in maintaining skin that is soft to the touch and pleasant on the eye. As well as having a good diet and avoiding excessive amounts of time in direct sunlight, using anti-aging creams, anti-wrinkle lotions and moisturizers can do wonders for your skin. If you suffer from any skin conditions, visit your local GP to see if he or she can prescribe anything or offer advice.

3. HAIR

If you're going to get a haircut specifically for your date, go for a style you feel comfortable with, rather than one from a magazine that you think men will like. The most important thing is to feel that you can be yourself around your date, and this may be hard if you're wearing a Brazillian style cut. If you suffer at all from facial hair, consider trying laser hair removal treatments. Mustaches seldom look sexy on men (with a few exceptions), and even worse for women.

4. CLOTHES

Once again, wear clothes that you feel comfortable wearing, both physically and emotionally. Most men enjoy the sight of a woman wearing a killer dress, but it is also the confidence with which she carries herself that can make all the difference. If you're happy wearing something low-cut, then be bold and go for it. If you'd feel more comfortable in something a little more conservative then wear that instead.

5. SHOES

This last tip may fall on deaf ears, but men don't care that much about shoes and would prefer you to be comfortable in a pair of sensible yet attractive shoes rather than in constant pain caused by 'killer heels'. Try to find a balance between aesthetic beauty and practicality.

Here's one problem that most women face when they're about to go out with an attractive guy: What to wear. Why is this an issue? Women, in general, think that they will get judged by the way they dress. They also want to give the best first impression possible. For these reasons, women agonize over their choice of clothes and accessories for hours before deciding on one outfit that best represents their true personality and good taste. Be confident in what you wear. Dress comfortably, but attractive, and don't spend so much time on your shoes, because I can assure you your date could care less.

CHAPTER 5

WHY IT'S OBVIOUS WHEN A GUY LIKES YOU

If you have ever thought if a guy you are interested in likes you at all, you are not alone. If you knew just a few behavioral tendencies, you might notice this in advance and you could come up with a complimenting strategy. In the end, I will give you one easy and practical way to test this theory.

EYE-CONTACT

Start observing how he looks at you. If you didn't know him before, he might be staring at you from a distance. And every time he notices that you look at him, he turns away. Men stare without making eye contact because they like what they see, but lack the confidence to speak up.

Commonly known - "the look" - when the guy sweeps his eyes from your head to your toes with a slight tentative smile, this obviously means that he is interested. Unfortunately, it may also mean he's just looking to get laid. Of course, if that is what you also want - go for it! But if you want something deeper - be careful.

If you already know him, it is easier to make eye-contact with him. It's said that a woman can read a man's heart through his eyes and no man can disguise his feelings if you make straight eye-contact with him. A guy who likes you will also try to make eye-contact with you.

BODY LANGUAGE

You can also notice which way the guy is standing when he is watching you or talking to you. Just check which way his feet are pointing. If both of his feet are pointing towards you, it means that he is comfortable with that direction and does not need to have an escape route. This could be a good indication that he might like you.

FRIENDS

Men don't usually tell you straight if they like you or not. However, if they are interested they will tell their best friends that they would like to know more about you. They might even get their friends on board to find out more about you. If you notice this happening, it is a sure sign.

CONVERSATION

When you get the chance to talk to him it is much easier to find out whether he likes you or not. If he can be relaxed and just himself when you are around, that means he's comfortable with you. If this doesn't mean anything else, then at least you can good friends. On the other hand, if he is instead looking away or not paying attention to what you say, and you get the feeling that he would rather be somewhere else – you're most likely right. A shy guy (and also not so shy if he has a crush on you) would be nervous and cannot always be so natural when talking to a woman. If he is interested he will still try make eye-contact, smile and talk about the things you are interested in.

If a guy likes you he also shows interest in things you like and do. My advice is that you try to get a conversation to an area you like and feel comfortable to talk about. For example, if you like cats, don't hesitate to say that. It doesn't matter if the guy doesn't like cats at all - he might just start comparing them to dogs (which means he has paid attention to what you have said and is interested in your point of view). Remember to listen also to what he has to say and let him talk!

BEHAVIOR

How does the guy treat you? Many guys (not all) playfully tease a girl they like. He might also be more polite to you than the other girls. He opens your door, takes your coat, gives you a chair, etc. Any behavior that is different to you than the others means that there is something special. This different behavior is an easy and good sign.

TESTING

One easy and practical way to test if he really is interested is just take an innocent step inside his personal space. If he steps away, he is not interested or he is a really shy person. If he is interested, he will set the boundaries of his personal space closer for you and will allow you to come closer than normal.

HERE ARE OTHER SIGNS THAT A GUY LIKES YOU

1. HE HANGS AROUND A LOT

When a guy always seems to hang around you and tends to gravitate back towards you when you move away, you have a fairly good indication that he likes you. Guys that like you will make the most of every opportunity to be with you. They will also make a habit of popping up at places and events where they know you are going to be.

2. HE MAKES AN EFFORT TO CONVERSE WITH YOU

If some random guy makes a comment to you (e.g. "Nice day, isn't it?") or comes over and starts a conversation with you, then this is a clear sign that he likes you or is at least interested in getting to know you. Yes, he may have a very plausible reason to talk to a stranger, such as wanting to know the time or needing directions, but you won't know until you continue the conversation.

This can also be a sign that a guy likes you if the guy is someone that you know, but not that well. For example, a guy who works on the same floor as you comes over and says "Hi" when you are at the coffee machine.

3. HE SEEMS NERVOUS AROUND YOU

For some reason when a guy likes you, he will often act all weird and isn't able to be himself. He will likely appear very nervous when he is around you. The most common sign of this is that he will smile too much and may even make weird comments. Other signs are that he might stutter, blush, or have trouble maintaining eye contact with you.

4. HE TRIES REALLY HARD TO KEEP A CONVERSATION WITH YOU GOING

When a guy likes you, he will usually take personal responsibility to keep a conversation with you going. As the conversational thread starts to die, he will tend to quickly try and save it, or even start a new thread before the dreaded awkward silence occurs.

5. HE TOUCHES YOU WITH HIS HAND AS HE IS TALKING

As a guy is talking to you, he might touch you on the back or shoulder with his hand, as he emphasizes a point. He may even stroke your hair briefly. You can interpret these as attempts by him to be a bit flirtatious with you, as it is not usually appropriate to touch someone like this unless you are romantically involved with them.

6. HE FLIRTS WITH YOU

There are many different ways that a guy can flirt with you. He might do it in a very subtle way, such as touching you on the shoulder as he is talking, like I mentioned above. Other forms of flirting include: smiling at you, teasing you, or yes, even making fun of you from time to time.

7. YOU RECEIVE A FACEBOOK FRIEND REQUEST FROM HIM, WHEN YOU DON'T KNOW HIM THAT WELL

This can be a fairly reliable sign if the guy has no mutual Facebook friends with you and would have had to do a lot of searching to find your profile. But it is a less reliable sign if he has a number of Facebook friends in common with you. This is because Facebook keeps firing friend suggestions at people, who are actually our friends' friends. Furthermore, a lot of people on Facebook try to add anyone they can to up their friend count.

So now you know what things you need to pay attention for to figure out if the guy likes you: the look, body language, their friends and how he pays attention to your interests and how he treats you. Don't stress over these things; pick one or two to keep an eye out for, and see what comes along.

CHAPTER 6

WHY IS HE EMOTIONALLY UNAVAILABLE?

Trying to have a relationship with an emotionally unavailable man can be very frustrating. Contrary to popular belief, just because someone is single does not mean they are emotionally available for a relationship. Just because someone is single does not mean they are relationship ready. Not everyone will be searching for their soul mate, or romantic partner, or even at all during this lifetime. They may very well be in a different place than you in their journey and truly may only be seeking a casual relationship.

There are also people that have absolutely no intention of being monogamous (even though they lie and say they are) who will simply never be emotionally available for you. There are many reasons why people will not be emotionally available for the type of relationship you are looking for. It is not always easy to spot an emotionally unavailable man.

He may very well present himself to you in such a way that it makes you believe he is ready for love. Everything may even be progressing along nicely. You are spending time together and he may very well be pursuing you... and you like it. You have been hesitant with your feelings and are keeping them in check, but he has insisted that you are the best thing ever. He may even talk about the connection the two of you share. When you finally give in and allow yourself to have an emotional connection to him, out come the signals of the unavailability.. he withdraws, he pulls back, he starts to cancel dates or fails to respond to calls or messages.

You are more confused than ever because he was the one who displayed the signs of being open emotionally.. but the instant you open up to him, the walls go up and the lines of communication go down. When the possibility of a real relationship became a reality to him, it was more than he could deal with... emotionally. As long as it was an idea, it was OK, but the reality of it caused him to bolt.

Before you let your heart invest in a relationship, you need to make sure the man you choose is emotionally available.

SIGNS OF EMOTIONALLY UNAVAILABLE MEN

1. Over-involvement in a career or in other people's lives. You want a man who has a purpose and reason for waking up each morning. He should ideally have a career that he enjoys and people who love and care about him. But too much involvement will be seen in that:

a. His career is all that he talks and thinks about: One of the signs of an emotionally unavailable man is that all he talks about is his career; his only interest is his career; he excels only in his career, and he has no other interest in life apart from his career. If you observe him carefully, you will realize that the only thing that he truly loves is his.. wait for it.. CAREER. In all practical ways, he is in love and married to his job. He may want you in his life so that you can meet those needs that his job does not, but his true love and the one that holds his emotions is his job. He breathes, sleep, dreams and fantasizes about his career; and you will always be a lower emotional priority in his life.

b. He is everyone's go-to guy: Yes you want a man who has friends and is involved in their lives, but one of the signs of emotionally unavailable men is their insatiable need to serve their friends and family members in every single little thing. It may seem like a cute trait at the beginning of the relationship when you think that he is one of the most giving men that you know, but it could be a sign of emotional unavailability. If he is at the beck and call of all his friends and relatives, then he will have minimal or no time for you. He simply does not have the time to be emotionally available to you. You may resent his friends or family members, but the problem may be him...not his friends or family members.

2. He has huge personal baggage: We all have baggage from our pasts. Nobody is spared from the hurt we can receive from others. But emotionally unavailable men have the type of baggage that cripples them emotionally. Whatever the past relationships did or did not do to them; emotionally unavailable men will react and treat you like the person or persons who hurt them in their past. He simply does not give you a chance to connect emotionally with him as he can only see you through the lenses of his past hurt.

3. He is just unable (or unwilling) to see the real you and so he creates (or sees) reasons why you are just like the people or person that hurt him in the past; and he disengages emotionally from you, ensuring that he can never be available to you when you need him to be. Some women find such men an irresistible challenge; they want to be the one that saves such a man and gets him to love again. But if you are one of those women then remember to tread carefully as this is a road full of incredible hurts and unless the man wants to change...all the love in the world may not be the proper course of action for them.

4. He has no real desire to be around you. A man who is emotionally unavailable also tends to be physically unavailable all the time. He may be in the same room or even sitting right next to you on the couch but his hands, eyes, and body never engage with you. He may go through the motions of living like eating; answer your questions with single answers or one liner's; have sex and do whatever you ask when at home. But he will not have any real interest in you and he will not cuddle, or hug you or touch you lightly as he talks. His interaction with you gives you the eerie feeling that he is thousands or even million of miles away from you, even when he is sitting or lying right next to you.

5. He has no interest in the things that are uniquely you or on issues that concern you. A man that is emotionally unavailable is living on autopilot, much like a robot. He functions by doing the minimal that he can in his relationship with you. He is not truly interested in your life and its unique twists and turns or in the things that you want him to do. He may get involved if you harass and nag him into action but generally, it is an uphill battle getting him involved in 'your' things. He may respond when you tell him about your day, but if you pay attention to him, his body and replies, you can almost hear them screaming their total disinterest in all that concerns you.

6. Your conversations are confined to the mundane life stuff. When a man is emotionally unavailable to you he talks to you about non-issues. He talks only when he must and he does not talk about himself or the things that are dear to his heart and life. Instead, he will talk about the weather, the traffic or other such life stuff; and how it was, without telling you how it

affected him or made him feel. He will talk like one who is an outside observer of his life.

His lack of emotional connection with you will make his conversation more like a commentary... like it happened, but not to him as he has no feelings about it that he cares enough to share with you.

7. Nothing about you and your life together gives him joy and happiness anymore (or so it seems that way). An emotionally unavailable man will not find you a source of pleasure. He may not be completely unhappy, but episodes of sheer delight and pleasure with you will be rare or non-existent... and you will know it.

8. He is an emotionally dead man only when he is around you: A man that is emotionally unavailable to you will display this action only when around you. When he is around other people he will be animated and engaged, and he will actually seem like a different man entirely. He will be passionate, engaged and happy around them. Do not believe the lie that it is because he has a passion for football or he has known the other people longer, etc. The truth is that he is not emotionally available to you.

These signs in combination with your intuition will let you know whether or not your man is emotionally unavailable to you. When you know that your man is emotionally unavailable, the next stage will be understood as to why he is disconnected from you. He may be going through a life crisis or he may just want out of the relationship.

Whichever the reson may be, it is imperative that you try your best not to take it personally. It may just be that he wans't ready for a commitment. Yea, it hurts, but this type of negative thinking will only create baggage and worry. This type of baggage can be carried on into your next relationship, and possibly ruin what could be a good thing. If this happens to you, understand that you are not alone and that it may not even be a reflection of you. Some individuals need to work on themselves before they can enjoy the company of others in a committed relationship.

SO WHAT CAN YOU DO?

The simplest and most clear answer to this is to distance yourself. But this is not easy to do for the majority of women out there, as some women feel that they can logically convince the guy to open up emotionally. This is just not possible for most, or at least sustainable for long periods of time.Therefore, it's very important for you to leave him alone and draw a line. If you don't let him know that you're not okay with him not being emotionally available to you right away, then you are only dragging things further which will lead to nothing but pain for both of you.

Infact, the major reason why you must draw the line and leave him alone for the time being is because once he knows that you are not okay with his actions, he will either change himself completely for you or you will finally know that he's just not someone you can spend the rest of your life with.

Emotionally unavailable men can turn your life upside down if you make the mistake of continuing to entertain the thought of being with them. They may present a challenge to some women or elevate the caring intuition in other women, but whatever emotions they evoke in you; know with certainty that loving them will be a journey to relationship hurts and heartbreaks.

CHAPTER 7

HEALTHY RELATIONSHIPS, NOT RELATIONSHITS.

There are many people whose preference is to have healthy relationships with the people in their lives; whether they are parent-child relationships, marriage or love relationships, family relationships, friendships, or even relationships with work colleagues. Building healthy relationships is a normal and natural desire. In fact, healthy relationships are a vital aspect of mental health, general health and wellness. So what do we need to know about building and maintaining healthy relationships?

Let us define some of the qualities of healthy relationships:

Each person takes responsibility for their own needs

You can easily discuss conflict and differences, without blame

The relationship is important to each person involved

Each person communicates openly and honestly

Abuse is absent; this includes physical, verbal, and emotional abuse

Each person has healthy boundaries -- can say "no" to requests without feelings of guilt

Certainly, it is important for each party in a relationship to understand, and be able to practice these aspects when interacting with others. It is my belief, however, that the key to healthy relationships is found, first, in our interactions with our Self, with

37

our Inner Being.

What is your relationship like with your Inner Being?

Are you in conflict with yourself?

Do you ever bring blame on yourself?

Do you get angry or frustrated with yourself?

Is your relationship with your Inner Being important to you?

Do you communicate openly and honestly with your Inner Being?

Do you abuse yourself; physically or with thoughts or words?

Can you follow your inner guidance without feeling guilty?

If your relationship with your Inner Being is not a healthy one, then keeping up a healthy relationship with others in your life could be challenging for you. The relationship you have with your Inner Being is the most important relationship you will ever have, and every other relationship is a reflection (in some way) of that most intimate, inner one.

Do you ever feel angry or frustrated with yourself, or blame and criticize yourself? Your Inner Being never argues with you, or blames you, or gets angry or frustrated or disappointed with you... your Inner Being always beams pure, positive, love and energy to you -- without exception. If you blame or criticize yourself, then you are in conflict with your Inner Being -- and you feel that tension through negative emotions.

Do you value your relationship with your Inner Being? Is it important to you to feel good and feel happy? When you value your relationship with your Inner Being, then you make every effort you can to feel happy, and to focus your attention on thoughts that feel good when you think them.

Do you communicate honestly and openly with your Inner Being? This is as easy as tuning into your emotions. Your emotions give you feedback about your relationship with your Inner Being...when you feel positive, happy emotions, you are in tune with youself. Negative emotions show that you are thinking of something that does not agree with what your Inner Being knows.

Do you take the time to nurture your relationship with your Inner Being? Do you nurture and soothe yourself? There are many ways you can nurture your spirit...you can meditate or listen to soothing music. You can also nurture yourself by thinking of someone you love, by taking a warm bath, by taking a walk, or by just giving yourself permission to chill... even if just for a moment.

Do you abuse yourself physically or with thoughts or words? It always feels good to receive support and encouragement from others...but we can also be supportive and encouraging toward ourselves. This can mean not asking or demanding too much of ourselves in time and effort -- by realizing that you don't have to do whatever-it-is this minute. We can applaud our efforts, and focus on what we did right (and not what went wrong).

HOW TO MAINTAIN A HEALTHY RELATIONSHIP

Maintaining a healthy relationship is key in the light of breakups and separation, which occurs frequently between boyfriends, girlfriends, and lovers; divorce, lawsuits, and issues with regard to single parenting that occurs between spouses, couples or partners is quickly becoming a growing concern among individuals and young couples. All those who are in troubled marriages or are in crisis-ridden relationships and affairs must endeavor to return back to learn and master the art of creating and maintaining a healthy relationship today rather than just throwing in the towel, quit or give up on their once beautiful, lovely, romantic and resourceful relationship.

Creating a healthy relationship and maintaining it is a matter of choice. It is about how prepared both of you are and how committed you are to work things out when it gets tough. To get you started, here are a few thought provoking tips on how to maintain a healthy relationship:

1. ALWAYS BE YOURSELF

You are wonderfully and uniquely made. If you find that you have to act or try to become someone you weren't born to be, in order to fulfill someone else's expectations, then something is seriously wrong. A true love will appreciate you for who you are and what you bring to the relationship, and vice-versa. If you feel as if you're being pressured to alter your character to do things you wouldn't usually do (drink, drugs, premature sex, lie) so that the person will continue to see you, that's a certain sign that things are unhealthy. Your true love will gladly embrace you just for who you are; so don't be afraid, step out on faith and show your true self.

2. DEVELOP DEEP COMMUNICATION WITH EACH OTHER

A healthy relationship goes much deeper than a surface affair. Even though you may both look good arm-in-arm, or standing next to each other, whether at a concert, family reunion, movie theater, or at church, can you talk when you're alone? What's going on in your conversations? Are they deep and meaningful or surface and bland? Do you discuss personal hopes, dreams, and goals, or just talk about the weather and the plot of the latest drama? Can you count on each other to lend a listening ear, good advice, and undivided attention? Good, honest, and deep conversation will keep you deeply connected. When in doubt, talk it out. Always keep the lines of communication open in your relationship.

3. DON'T IGNORE, BUT EXPLORE YOUR DIFFERENCES

Do your personalities blend well? Is one of you on the optimistic path while the other is on the pessimistic side of the road? Opposites may initially attract, but eventually, they can repel each other. It's important that your personalities are compatible. If one views life through rose colored glasses, while the other is always singing-the-blues, then you have to make some sort of adjustment to accommodate each other. The simple truth is oil and vinegar make an excellent salad dressing, but they don't mix well in romantic relationships, unless both personalities can explore each other and find some sort of balance. If you can adjust and love each other's personality, regardless of any differences, and bring out the best when you're together, then this is a winning combo, and you could very well be a dynamic duo in a lifelong healthy relationship.

4. SHARE SIMILAR INTEREST AND VALUES

You don't have to have the same exact interests. As a matter of fact, having diverse preferences can help you to share new and exciting

41

things with each other. However, make sure you have at least a few common interests, so it won't be an ongoing battle over what to do and where to go to keep you both satisfied. You may have to compromise in some areas like sports, politics, movies, shopping, music, etc. Keep in mind that compromising doesn't mean depriving each other of their individual interests, but instead it means participating in each other's interests.

5. DISCUSS YOUR SPIRITUAL BELIEFS TOGETHER

If you're not on the common ground with your beliefs about who and what God means to each of you (or lack of), this will eventually cause a rift in your relationship. Don't try to conceal your true beliefs and hope that it will all just one day fall into place; it won't. Make sure you talk about your faith honestly and openly with each other.

6. APPRECIATE EACH OTHER'S UNIQUE BODY TEMPLE

Let's face it, we're all built differently. We come in a variety of shapes, sizes, and shades. In order to have a healthy physical and emotional relationship, you must embrace and appreciate each other's total package. One of the worse things a couple can do to each other is to fantasize or try to fit their partner into someone else's body image. When you throw away the preconceived "ideal body type" perceptions, you'll enjoy the true worth of your partner.

7. TALK ABOUT SEX AND MONEY

Two of the biggest destroyers of healthy relationships are the misuse, abuse, lack of or over-use of sex and money. Both are very important and very personal in your love life. Yet, unfortunately, most couples make the mistake of not setting quality time aside early in their relationship to discuss these two vital components. To put it bluntly, "You've got to know where you're heading before you get to the bedding; and know what you're spending before it gets beyond mending."

In deep romantic relationships, there is a world of difference between "having sex" and "making love," just as there is a major difference between being "involved" and "being in love." The misuse of sex, just like the misuse of money, can cause major turbulence in a relationship. These can be dangerous influences which can overwhelm your relationship, or they can be healthy tools for intimacy and success. It's up to both you and your partner to know what sex and money mean to each of you and to make sure that you share your beliefs and feelings with each other. Otherwise, both the sex and money issues can become major conflicts which can destroy even the deepest love.

8. TRY TO GET ALONG WITH EACH OTHER'S FRIENDS AND FAMILIES

Although your happiness ultimately depends on how well the two of you get along with each other, some input from loved ones can be the frosting on the cake. Do you have a healthy interaction with each other's close associates? Make sure you ask some supportive family members and/or dear friends of their opinion about your choice in pursuing their loved one. If the advice is not what you want to hear, examine it closely, evaluate the source, think about it, and make up your own mind anyway. Make sure you also meet your partner's family and closest friends, and discreetly observe their interactions with each other. Look to see if there is any dysfunctional family pattern that you need to address or get help with. There is an old saying, "Show me your company, I'll tell you who you are." Chances are, if your partner has a healthy interaction with loved ones, you will also get the same treatment--and much more!

9. STAY AWAY FROM NEGATIVE PEOPLE

It's important to make a special note here, that although the interactions of relatives and friends can be a plus in building a healthy relationship, some, unfortunately, can also be a minus. If you face unhealthy interference and discouragement from loved ones because of their personal insecurities, don't let them have any influence in your relationship. Both you and your partner must be on the same page and decide to keep negative people out of your personal love life in order to love and grow together in a harmonious, healthy relationship.

10. LEARN TO LAUGH TOGETHER

This one doesn't need much explanation; if there's no joy, there's very little hope. Laughter keeps love alive. Find something that you can both get a good hearty laugh from. Here's a little secret that works wonders: A good sense of humor and a pleasant disposition has a magnetic attraction that makes people always want to be in your presence. How can that special person resist your gorgeous smile and sparkling eyes? Go ahead, laugh a bit--have fun and enjoy.

A healthy relationship is one where the two of you can be yourselves and have nothing to hide about. A healthy relationship is one where there is general support. It is not about every man or woman for themself. In healthy relationships, couples support each other in all ways. Be it financially, physically, emotionally and any kind of support that is needed. No one in the relationship should be afraid to ask for help just because they think they will look weak and the partner might end up looking down upon them. Everyone needs help once in a while, even the strongest ones sometimes need help. A healthy relationship is one where a partner is not afraid to ask for it and will not feel guilty about asking for it; nor will they feel like they are disturbing their partner. That is as long as it is something you really need help with.

A healthy relationship is rare these days. Many of us have forgotten what it means to have one. Reminding ourselves of these healthy relationship tips will make our current relationships better than ever.

CHAPTER 8

CHIVALRY IS NOT DEAD YET, APPRECIATE THE LITTLE THINGS

Chivalry is not dead. It is still quivering with anticipation somewhere, waiting to be engaged in service. However, it is being suppressed by each of the following:

1. Equality of the sexes: May younger women no longer wish to have anything done on their behalf, no matter how simple. There is the misguided notion that every male who might wish to do something for a woman, because he admires her or just wishes to be courteous, has an ulterior motive. Women feel increasingly compromised or obliged by such actions and so there are fewer opportunities to be chivalrous. Don't let this be you. Appreciate the ones who open doors for you or offer small favors. It doesn't mean they're automatically looking for sex, it's very possible they're just being nice, as it's how they were raised.

2. Distrust and Suspicion: Everyone comes under the spotlight as being guilty before being innocent these days. We no longer accept behavior at face value, especially when it comes from the opposite sex. We tend to question attitude, motives, and actions much more than we used to do which then demotivates men to do anything at all for fear of being negatively labeled or rejected. Just take a breath, relax, and look at the situation from an analytical, logical, and non fallacious point of view. Keep emotion out of it and judge something by fact, not opinion.

3. Lack of personal confidence and self esteem: People who are low in esteem may be unsure as to how to handle chivalrous acts. They feel embarrassed by compliments; they tend to focus on themselves and are also not sure how to react in the face of any chivalry. Many people lack self-love and so, when they are treated in very caring ways, they are apt to doubt the sincerity of the giver. Not used to giving to themselves, and more likely to be self-conscious, low confidence people are likely to ignore chivalrous acts or to interpret them as suspicious.

4. The age we live in: There is far less emphasis on 'gentlemanly' qualities these days. Young boys are brought up just to be themselves, no longer as 'gentlemen', a state which is now more familiar to older men and to which they used to aspire. The social protocol of behaving like a gentleman and being there for a lady has been lost in many parts of the world. With it goes the kind of actions that demarcated gentlemen and made them much sought after. The days of standing up when a woman enters the room, holding doors, and pushing in chairs have been on the decline for years.

Chivalry is still there smoldering in many corners, but, as with everything in society, we have to accept that the interpretation of what it means to be chivalrous can also change and be dictated by the expectations of the age we are in.

CHAPTER 9
WHY DO MEN CHEAT?

According to statistics, reports show that men cheat more than a woman (or are just caught more often). This may or may not be surprising to you. The question here is why. This is not something that has been definitely nailed down, but there is one reason that seems to stand out from the rest. Read on to find out the most common reason that men cheat in relationships.

THE REASON

Most women tend to feel it is their fault that their man is cheating. This leads to the woman feeling bad about herself and causes problems with self-esteem. The truth is that the top reason men cheat have nothing to do with the woman they are with. The most common reason that men cheat is that men have a natural drive to seek out various sexual partners. They may seek out someone who has a quality their current partner lacks, but draws them in.

Men seem to be biologically inclined to cheat. It is controllable, though, since there are many men that do not cheat. However, for some men, this biological draw is too strong for them to handle. They may not even mean to hurt the woman they are with, but that is always what seems to happen. Does this mean they should get a free pass? Absolutely not.

HOW TO SPOT CHEATING

Spotting cheating is not always easy. It can be made difficult if the man has cheated before. However, there is some truth to the old saying once a cheater, always a cheater, because once a man gives into the natural tendency, they may have a hard time deflecting it in the future. Usually, you will have a feeling or see changes in your partner that signal he is cheating. You may even see obvious signs such as lipstick stains on clothing or the smell of strange perfume. You may even get calls from his mistress. Sometimes a mistress will actually talk to you and tell you what is going on and other times they can simply hang up.

HOW TO DEAL WITH CHEATING?

When you suspect that your man is cheating, you need to deal with it. Now, I'm not saying you need to bring him onto some lousy talk show or have a radio host confront him about your suspicions.. You have to gather proof or facts and bring them up in a respectful matter. Also, you need to make sure that you are prepared to handle what comes after you get him to admit he has cheated.

Before you confront him, you need to realize that he may try to explain away all his actions and the proof you have. Either this, or he may flat out tell you the truth. Please keep in mind that just because you suspect something, doesn't mean it's actually happening. Hear him out and form your own LOGICAL (not emotional) conclusions. You have to be ready to either counter these and get to the truth, or accept them at face value. I know these ideas are not easy to implement, but they are doable. It will take commitment on your part to get to know these materials..

CHAPTER 10

PHYSICAL AND EMOTIONAL ATTRACTIVENESS

Physical attraction is important. Not only in the sense that men are visual learners and it helps to look good to get their attention, but because it will boost your self confidence as well. However, just looking pretty alone will not keep his interest for very long.

The attraction goes a whole lot deeper than just looking good. I am sure that you have noticed that there are many gorgeous women who always seem to be having relationship problems, so clearly looking good isn't the only thing to do with having a lasting, healthy, happy relationship. The attraction a man has for you is nothing that he can control either. In other words, he will either feel it for you or he won't. Unfortunately, there is no middle ground with this one.

Because it is nothing that he can control, women can use that knowledge to their advantage!

So what kind of attraction do you need to build with the man in your life and how do you do that? You need to build massive emotional attraction with him. This is how you inspire a man to be interested in being with you and only you. The emotional attraction you build with him has to do with how you make him feel when he is around you.

In essence, you have to make him feel good when around you so that he has fun when he is with you and remembers the good times you spent together when he is away from you. That way when he is away from you, he keeps thinking about you and every time he thinks of you, he cannot help but smile and wonder when the next time is that he will be able to talk to you or see you.

It's easy to build this attraction if you remember that if he feels good being with you, he will stay. If he feels bad being with you, he will go (and sometimes faster than you can blink).

SO HOW DO YOU BUILD EMOTIONAL ATTRACTION WITH A MAN?

1. Play with him: Make sure that you have lots of fun together. Always keep him smiling. When he is smiling, everything is good. This tip may sound incredibly simplistic, but it is really very powerful.

2. Give him as much space as you can. Enjoy the time you have when you are together. Have fun and live in the moment, but do not crowd him. Pull back sometimes and allow him to miss you, to wonder about you and to come looking for you. Let him have fun with that sometimes. Enjoy the magic when he finds you.

3. Be interesting and unpredictable. Be provocative, sometimes with what you say and do so that he never quite knows what you will say or do next. That way he cannot help but think about you because you keep him guessing.

4. Take things slow. It doesn't matter how much fun you are having with him; do not try to rush ahead by forcing your feelings on him. The key here is staying one step behind him and two steps ahead. This is how you keep him on his toes.

Building emotional attraction is as much fun for you as it is for him and in the end, you both get what you want.

HOW CAN YOU STOP NAGGING? TIPS FOR MEN AND WOMEN

Nagging: "To be a persistent source of annoyance or distraction. To irritate by constant scolding or urging." That is the definition from Merriam-Webster.

This is what an individual feels when they think they are being "nagged". Who wants to deal with the constant annoyance and scolding? Not any grown adult I know. So what is the root of nagging? Depending on where you look, you may find different answers, but from what I've learned, nagging is a result of a lack of communication between two partners.

It is a way for one person to actually elicit a response from the other, albeit a negative response. When one partner feels like communication is failing, and they need some sort of interaction from their other half, they resort to any means necessary to get some interaction.

Nagging is one way to achieve this. They ride you and pester you until finally, you retaliate with anger and frustration. It worked for them; they got you to say something. They now know you are listening to them, and that's really all they wanted. They wanted some attention, to know you hear them. What they hope for is a positive exchange between the two of you, and feel that negative communication is better than no communication.

Everyone has a need to feel wanted, needed, and important to someone else. That is a big reason why we choose to be with our spouse in the first place. We love that they care for us, want to be with us, understand us, and want to grow with us. When those feelings subside, we begin to feel very insecure. We miss the interaction, compassion, conversation and love that we grew so accustomed to. We crave that energy, and we want it back. Instead of expressing that we need attention, we can fall into the nagging phase. Afraid to rock the boat more permanently, we feel nagging is more short term. So we nag until we get the same response (attention) from our spouse. And this leads to a fight or argument and snowballs the feelings of insecurity on both parties.

Can nagging, then, lead to an affair? The answer is absolute yes! And the affair could come from either spouse. This is because when nagging occurs, it is a sign that the basic needs of husband and wife (or boyfriend and girlfriend) are not being met. You are not giving your spouse the attention they need, the feeling of security, and so on and so forth.

Likewise, they feel that you are not providing them with those same needs, and thus they nag you until you come through for them. When basic needs aren't being met, physically or emotionally, a spouse will seek alternative means to satisfy those needs. This is how affairs happen. If you fail to pay attention to your spouse, show sincere interest in them, and let them know how important you are to them, they will find someone who can provide these essential needs. This may come in the form of emotional cheating or physical cheating.

How can you overcome this? I suggest you each sit down (individually) and write down what "your" marriage profile is. A marriage profile is simply what you expect your marriage to be like. Start out from the time you wake up until the time you go to bed.

Describe how your ideal day would go and where and how your spouse is included in that day. If your spouse isn't included, then that's another problem in itself.

Ask yourself these questions along the way:

Do you share a meaningful conversation with your spouse when you wake up or do you just get ready for work?

Do you eat meals together? Home or Out?

Do you call your spouse throughout the day or just wait until you get home?

Do you think about your spouse during the day?

Do you plan what you and your spouse will do later during the day or week? Any dates with your spouse?

What do your conversations consist of?

How many minutes during the day are you sharing meaningful conversation with your spouse?

What activities do you do with your spouse?

How do you end your evening with your spouse?

Do you have a meaningful conversation before bed?

How happy are you after this "ideal" day?

Writing these things out and creating a profile is essential to happiness. Now, see what your spouse has written and compare.

This type of activity will create meaningful conversation and ideally bring back the spark you are missing. Constant nagging is a sign that something is wrong in your relationship, and you need to address it before one partner decides to either have an affair or end it. You just learned a great exercise to help build a better, more trusting relationship with your partner. Practice this exercise and you can help eliminate nagging in your relationship.

CONCLUSION

Does your man seem disinterested when you are trying to talk to him about something vital to you? Do you feel that you too have a problem and you wish to discuss it? Does your man seem less than excited when you insist you both must talk about the issue right then and there?

Men, more often than not, wish to keep their problems to themselves and think about them for a while. It does not mean your man is incapable of communicating with you, it just means that he would rather process the situation before saying anything. More often than not, a man will need to come up with something concrete to say or a specific solution to a problem, rather than just discussing several different options with you. Though women often think about their problems out loud and wish to discuss or talk about every aspect of an issue, it does not mean men have to do the same. When it comes to communicating, give your man some space. When he is ready to talk to you about an issue, permit him to approach you. Remind yourself that you are two different creatures and when it comes down to it, men and women have a very different style of communication. Sometimes, talking about an issue isn't always the best way to resolve it. Sometimes, the best response to a problem is time.

Do not be offended when you don't get exactly the response you would expect or desire. Guys are not easy to figure out at first. The next time you are upset with your man, try to think about it the way he would. Simply acknowledging that men think in different ways can lift off a heavy burden from your shoulders. The next time he reacts differently to what you would expect, don't sweat the small stuff. It doesn't mean that he doesn't care. He just thinks differently than the way you do.

Understanding men really isn't all that complicated when you break it down this way. It truly is a matter of widening your horizons and accepting another person's point of view. Once you can accept that, you'll be well on your way to having a relationship that has a true chance of succeeding.

SOME FINAL THOUGHTS

Bad Boys

Just stop chasing the bad boys. Yes, almost every girl goes through a bad boy phase where they love the thrill of dating that one guy who gets in trouble or hangs out with the tough crowd. It's not worth it, nor does it make you look cool. Don't justify it by convincing yourself that you can change him. Maybe you can, but in the end it may just be a wasted few years of life before you realize you left a lot of decent guys on the sidelines, while trying to straighten out that mess you started dating in high school. Just get it out of your system early and move on.

He Looked at Another Girl!

Ladies.. Just because your man looks or glances at another woman passing by, does not mean he's being unfaithful or wants to run over and pounce on her. It is in no way meant to be a sign of disrespect to you or an insult in any way when he does this. Everyone can appreciate a good looking individual, and let's face it, there are better looking people in the world than the one you're dating. It's okay for women to look at guys, and for guys to look at women. As the old saying goes "It's okay to look at the menu, as long as you eat at home".

Spell it out for Him

In reality, some guys just don't get it. They may never understand you, and in turn, it makes it that much more difficult for you to understand them. To some guys, you might as well be the equivalent of solving a Rubik's cube behind your back with your hands cuffed in front of you while a foreigner is yelling at you in another language. To many guys, this is how it is. Help him out; spell it out for him. Tell him what you like and don't like. Tell them what your expectations are and don't keep him guessing if it's clearly not working.

The First Move

I get it, traditionally speaking, the guy is supposed to make the first move. Now, this may come as a surprise to some but NOT ALL GUYS ARE CONFIDENT (yes, that was sarcastic). If you're interested, just help the poor guy out and kiss him already. This may just be what he needed to spark his confidence. Don't wait days or weeks for him to do something he clearly wants to do but is too afraid for fear of getting slapped or rejected because he's too naïve to read the obvious signs in front of him. Don't beat around the bush; be blunt with what you want. Sometimes, you'll know it before he does. This goes for both sides of the relationship.

With that being said, have fun in a relationship. If it stops being fun, find out why and try to fix it. It's a two-way street and it works both ways. If it's still not working, move on. There are plenty of fish in the sea and believe it or not, there are loads of people out there that you would be completely and utterly happy to fall in love and spend the rest of your life with.

Made in the USA
Middletown, DE
10 April 2023

28546143R00035